DIHLM

BI 3318997 8

KU-545-445

 LIBRARY SERVICES

FOR REFERENCE ONLY

NOT TO BE
TAKEN AWAY

EMPLOYABILITY

FACTOR

DO YOU KNOW WHAT IT TAKES TO GET THE JOB?

BY

JILL RUSSELL

authorHOUSE™

1663 LIBERTY DRIVE, SUITE 200
BLOOMINGTON, INDIANA 47403
(800) 839-8640
WWW.AUTHORHOUSE.COM

No part of this book may be reproduced, stored in a retrieval system, or transmitted by any means without the written permission of the author.

First published by AuthorHouse 02/18/05

ISBN: 1-4208-2025-7 (sc)

Printed in the United States of America
Bloomington, Indiana

This book is printed on acid-free paper.

FORWARD

I heard Andrew Young, whose accomplishments include former Civil Rights Leader, Mayor of Atlanta, United States Congressman and United Nations Representative, speak several years ago and he told a compelling story from the civil rights movement during the 1960's. This story has stayed with me since that night and I would like to share it with you. I pray that it causes you to think seriously about the choices that you make in your life from day to day that not only jeopardize the opportunities of your *present*, but may have ramifications that affect the entire direction of your *future*.

The story is as follows. During the early formation of the civil rights movement, it was necessary to elect a figurehead or spokesperson so that the world would be able to have a recognizable face to identify with the movement. The elders, Andrew Young being one, came together and selected the man whom they felt was the most qualified to take on this very prestigious yet challenging position. When they arrived at the home of their first choice for the position, he was drunk. They withdrew the nomination from him and gave it to a virtually unknown young man named Martin Luther King Jr.

Life is about making choices. That first young man, whose name Andrew Young did not divulge, made the choice to get drunk and the consequence of that *one* decision was not only that he would hold no leadership position in the civil rights movement but ultimately have no holiday named after him, no historical landmark dedicated to him, no libraries, museums or schools that would bare his name. One foolish choice on an ordinary evening had extraordinary consequences and ultimately left this man with no worldwide honor or recognition but the legacy of Martin Luther King Jr. remains to this day.

Most of the choices that you make, good or bad, will probably not have the historic consequences that this young man had to live with. However, your life and even the lives of the generations that come after you are affected by the day-to-day choices that you make in relationships, education, finance, health and everything in between. Looking back over my life, I can identify poor choices that I made that negatively impacted my life for years after the decision was made. Both of these decisions were educational and financial. Two of the worst choices that I made were in college. I did not take my studies seriously and I did not take the repayment of my student loan seriously. These choices were defining moments in my life. Of course, I did not realize the significance of the impact of the consequences until I was much older. Consequences that included having to settle for low paying jobs, struggling to pay bills, a terrible credit rating, not being able to purchase a home or a car and not being able to get a checking or a savings account. I spent most of my young adult life in that situation. I waited tables, washed windows, threw newspapers and pawned jewelry to make ends meet. Poor choices make life more challenging than it has to be. It was not until I was in my early thirties that I began to get fed up with my paycheck-to-paycheck existence and began to plan, again, for my future. It did not happen overnight. I worked the worst shifts. I worked weekends and holidays. At times I worked three jobs. In a matter of a few years I went from making six dollars an hour to making $40,000 a year with two weeks vacation, sick days and annual bonuses in addition to medical and dental insurance by working hard and advancing within the company. This may seem like a lot to some and it may seem like a starting place for others but the point is this, whether you start at six dollars an hour or forty thousand dollars a year, there are always opportunities for advancement. With the opportunity of financial advancement that I received, that was all that I needed to pay off my debt, get my credit report cleaned up, buy a house and start thinking about what I *really want to do with my life.*

Throughout this book I have included brief biographies of people who have started out with very little and through persistence, determination and purposing to do better, they have become very successful. You may be thinking, "What does this have to do with getting a job"? My desire is not only to help you get a job, but to encourage you to excel in life. I want you to fulfill your dreams. If you do not already have a direction that you want to go in or something that you want to do with your life, I want you to be encouraged to dream big and to work hard to see that dream come true. When we were younger we all had wonderful ideas of what we wanted to do with our life. We were going to do everything from being a doctor, a fireman, a lawyer, a singer, to owning our own business. Somewhere along the line, the circumstances of our life, mixed in with a few poor choices here and there, and we find ourselves so far removed from what we wanted to be when we grew up. Maybe we will never have the career that we dreamed about at the age eight or even eighteen. But dreaming new dreams and redefining goals can be done at any age. It may even be that a serious career in any given field is no longer your hearts desire. You may simply want a stable job with a solid company that has health benefits so that you can care for and support your family. No matter what your long-term goal may be, having a job, even if it pays less than what you feel that you are worth, is the foundation upon which you can pursue your dreams.

I am sensitive to the fact that being unemployed has many consequences. I am aware of the seriousness of the situation that you find yourself in at this time in your life. Any period of unemployment be it brief or be it long, can affect your immediate, present financial situation and possibly long term financial situation as bills are not met, bill collectors start calling, credit reports are damaged, savings accounts are tapped, 401k's are drained and tension builds up in the home between spouses. I understand that for many men your ego is tied up in your ability to provide for your family, likewise women, many of you are the primary providers for your family. Although there are many variables to all of our life experiences, the impact of unemployment is more complex than *not having a job.* Every person I interview, I understand that they need me to give them a job to circumvent many of the issues that I just described. The majority of the people that I interview I cannot offer them a job. For the most part, many of the reasons that I did not select a particular applicant to work for my company was because they lacked the knowledge of what the Human Resource Manager is looking for that has nothing to do with education or experience.

The reason why I am writing this book is to give you inside information concerning what employers are looking for *and* looking at when they are hiring. I call it the Employability Factor or the E-Factor. With this insight, you can set yourself apart from the masses, get the job and achieve your goals. Whether you are applying for your first job at a store in the mall or fast food restaurant, office receptionist, have been laid off or fired and need to make a career change, seeking to intern with a company that may possibly hire you upon completing your college education, or looking for better career opportunities, knowing the E-Factor is your key to success. It will not only increase your opportunity in being selected to work for a company, but may also open doors within that company for advancement.

This book gives you clear insight into the job market from an employer's perspective. You will receive practical instruction on appearance, attitude and etiquette, resume writing, filling out an application and interview skills. Your success in all of these categories will be what employers will use to rate your Employability Factor.

In addition to this, I will address how a strong work ethic opens opportunities for advancement and much, much more. There are great things in store for you in your life and I hope that this book helps you take one small step on that journey towards success.

TABLE OF CONTENTS

INTRODUCTION

After years of working in the Human Resource department of a company that has over eight hundred employees, and interviewing on average thirty people a day, I am convinced that too many people do not know *how* to get a job. The "how to" of getting a job is what I call the Employability Factor or the E-Factor. Having a college degree or specialized education does not necessarily mean that *you* will be the one that is selected. There are many companies that are willing to train the right candidate. Most people fail in their job search for a variety of reasons that include dressing unprofessionally when applying for the job, not using professional communication skills, not filling out the application fully and properly, not having a professional response to the questions asked in the interview, wanting to get paid more money than the company is willing or able to offer, or having a poor employment history.

Many times I have stopped the interview process to instruct an applicant on what they are doing wrong so that they may possibly learn from the experience and succeed in the next interview. Not many people who work in the Human Resource department of a company would take the time to give you practical instruction so that you have an opportunity succeed. They would simply give you a polite "Don't call us we'll call you". However, I sincerely care about the welfare of the people who come into my office and need a job. I remember what it was like putting in applications all over town and desperately waiting for a call back. One thing that I did not know then but do fully understand now is that when there is an advertisement for "available positions", for every position that a company is hiring for the Human Resource manager usually interviews up to fifty people per position. That means if you do not make a *great* first impression, your application will never be considered for a position within the company. Knowing the E-Factor is your key to success.

So how do you set yourself apart from the crowd and keep your application out of the abyss of rejects? Keep reading the book and apply the information as to what employers are looking for *and* looking at while you are on your job search. It will make the difference between you calling endlessly with the same old line…"I am checking on the status of my application"… and the employer actually calling to offer *you* a job.

CHAPTER 1

PROFESSIONAL APPEARANCE

<u>Madame C.J. Walker</u>

Born Sarah Breedlove in 1869 on a Louisiana plantation, this daughter of a former slave transformed herself from an uneducated farm laborer and laundress into a successful, self-made entrepreneur. She often said, "I got my start by giving myself a start". During the 1890's Sarah began to suffer from a scalp ailment that caused her to lose most of her hair. She experimented with homemade remedies and created a product that helped her ailment. With that knowledge, she founded her own business selling *Madame C.J. Walker's Wonderful Hair Grower*. To promote her new products, she began selling them door-to-door in addition to demonstrating the scalp treatments at churches and lodges. By 1910, with creative sales and marketing strategies she had parlayed her invention into a successful business. Madame Walker once said, "There is no royal flower-strewn path to success. And if there is, I have not seen it. For if I have accomplished anything in life, it is because I have been willing to work hard".

Professional Appearance

Have you ever heard the saying "First impressions are everything"? Well, 99% of the time that is absolutely true. I can usually determine when a person enters our office to fill out an application, based upon how they are dressed and if their communication is professional and polite, if I would consider them for a position with our company. I will address the need for professional and polite communication skills in the next chapter. I want to devote this chapter entirely to the Employability Factor of having a professional appearance.

Why is a professional appearance so important when seeking employment? When you respond to an advertisement for a position with a company, *you* are looking for a job and *they* are looking for an individual to represent their company. In business, image is everything. Whether it is retail, fast food, industrial or corporate America, you are their direct contact with the public, their customers and or clients. If you wear their logo on a uniform, you are literally a walking advertisement. Now granted there are jobs that you can find that do not care about how you dress, how many visible tattoos you have or how you wear your hair. Most of these jobs are going to pay you minimum wage while offering no job stability, no benefits and no opportunity for advancement. The goal of this book is not to help you get *any* job. Although having a low paying job is better than having no job at all. I really want you to have a good paying job with opportunities for advancement. The better you understand how a professional appearance plays a major role in job opportunities the better off you will be in getting the job you want.

Again, first impressions are everything and it starts the moment that you walk in the door. Never think that you are only filling out the application so it does not matter what you wear. Sometimes employers conduct on-the-spot interviews. If you have come in dressed too casual, that is your first impression. Even if the Human Resource Manager does not meet with you when you fill out the application, the person giving you the application may write notes on the application concerning your professional appearance and or manners and this may affect your opportunity for receiving a call to set up a formal interview if your appearance is not professional.

There is a fundamental difference between what is considered appropriate professional attire for women verses men, I will address these differences separately beginning with the women. But first let me address some appearance issues that could affect male or female.

I realize that in some social circles it is culturally "hip" to have visible tattoos, facial piercing and or gold teeth. What I mean by "visible" tattoos is tattoos that are on the neck, forearm, wrist, etc. This *does* hinder you from obtaining certain jobs. You may be thinking that there are jobs that would take you just the way you are. To that I would say that you are correct. I would also say that most of those jobs would also pay you minimum wage with no health insurance, paid vacation or opportunity for advancement. Are there some jobs that may pay a reasonable wage with reasonable benefits? Sure there are, but why limit yourself? Who is to say that *that* employer is going to hire *you*? I understand the desire to want to express you individuality, but do not make choices concerning your appearance that may hinder your opportunities in getting a job. An attitude that says "This is ME…take it or leave it" may only leave you unemployed, screening the phone for bill collectors, and parking your car at a friend's house so the "REPO" man cannot take your car.

If you do not have visible tattoos, facial piercing or gold teeth, by all means, with the understanding that it may hinder you from getting a job, please think twice before you do. If you already have any of the above, when you are looking for a job I would suggest that you do the following: If you have visible tattoos, dress in a manner that would cover them as best as possible even in the summer months; If you have any visible piercing other than your ears (men, absolutely no earrings) you need to take it out prior to filling out the application. That means any lip, eyebrow, nose or tongue piercing. And no you cannot hide the tongue piercing. Employers see it when you talk and often hear it click against your teeth. If you have gold teeth, there is not a whole lot that you can do about it. One gold tooth is not considered *that* unprofessional but when you have two or more and one of them is engraved with a martini glass you are really pushing your luck with many employers. My suggestion is to smile with your mouth closed.

Lastly, there are a few miscellaneous issues I would like to address. Do not wear too much perfume or cologne. The office where you are interviewing is generally very small and heavy perfume or cologne lingers long after you leave. The person who interviews you does not want to suffer with your preferred scent for the rest of the day. And by all means, take off the sunglasses once you enter the office. This does not make you look "cool" or "intriguing" it only makes you look unprofessional.

Do you see where I am going with this? All of these details make a difference when applying for a job. Nothing that I am saying is meant to offend or discourage anyone who may fall into one or more than one of the categories that I would say "don't do". I want you to be completely aware of the E-Factor of what many employers look at *and* look for upon consideration for hire so that you can be prepared. Some of the instruction that I offer may seem trivial to you, but I guarantee that an employer does not see it as trivial. Everything counts. So with that said, let's continue with separate appearance issues for woman and men beginning with the women.

WOMEN

CLOTHING

Ladies, ladies, ladies. The most important thing for you to keep in mind when you are applying for a job is that you are not auditioning for a part in a MTV or BET dance video. That means, leave the short skirts, halter-tops, crop tops, stretch pants at home. Even during the summer months, this is *not* appropriate attire for an interview. If you walk in my office showing bare shoulders and back, bare midriff, most of your thigh and half of your breasts, I can guarantee that you are *not* going to get the job. Yes, I know what you're thinking, "A woman may not hire me but a man sure will". Well, think again sister. A man would not hire you either because you look like you are a sexual harassment case waiting to happen and that means you are potentially more trouble than you are worth.

You do not have to dress so conservative that it does not reflect your personal style, but you do need to dress professionally. So not only does that mean leave the "I-look-so-hot-in-this" outfit at home it also means that you cannot show up in sweats or jeans and a T-shirt. Remember, you are trying to get a job and you will be filling out your application along side many other applicants who are dressed professionally. If that is the case, you will probably never be considered for hire if you do not dress the same or better.

I have told you what not to wear. So what is appropriate attire? It really is very simple… wear a dress, suit, skirt or slacks and a blouse. If you do not have anything that fits that description, I highly recommend that you get something. That may mean that you need to go purchase a new outfit. I do understand that you may not have the money at this time to invest in a new outfit. If that is the case, my recommendation is that you borrow something from a roommate, friend or family member. When I interviewed with the company that I now work for, I had to borrow a suit from a friend because I did not have anything that was appropriate. I had worked as a waitress for years and always wore a uniform so all the clothes in my closet were too casual for a job interview. I borrowed something to wear for that interview and I got the job! Fortunately *that* position required me to wear a uniform also because I only had the one outfit and I had to return it to my friend the next day. But a year later when I was promoted to a new position that allowed me to wear my own clothes, I was desperate because I did not have any clothes to wear in a professional setting. So what do you do when you need professional clothes but have little to no money? Thrift store!! Yes, I did say thrift store. Why not? You can find great looks at next to nothing prices. Now it does take time and patience to go through the racks of clothes but the rewards are worth the effort. If you do not have any professional business clothes in your closet and you have little money in your pocketbook, your best alternative is a thrift store. Having a professional appearance is the first of many criteria of the E-Factor that you will be evaluated on when meeting with an employer.

If you already have a job and you are going to fill out an application for another job, whether you are looking for a second job or looking to leave your present job, you must still dress professionally even if you are going to fill out the application on your lunch break or after work. I have interviewed many people who are either in uniforms for other companies or work industrial or construction jobs and come into the office in dirty clothes and worn out uniforms. I know that you may be hard working and your time may be limited but many employers will view your appearance as "sloppy" and not consider you for a position. If there is no other way, based upon your busy work schedule and the hours that a specific company accepts applications you may have to come straight from work. In that case, if you cannot change your clothes in a restroom, be as clean and pressed as possible. It is important that you tell the receptionist, in addition to the person interviewing you, if you do receive an interview that day, that you apologize for not being dressed appropriately but you were only able to fill out the application on your lunch break or after work whichever the case may be. This simple explanation will let the person interviewing you know that you do understand the difference between professional and unprofessional attire and they will not hold it against you in their decision making process.

HAIR

Now that you have the right clothes on, let's talk about the hair. It is important that your hair is neat and clean. I know that this seems like common sense, but you would be surprised at how many women come into my office looking as if they just woke up. Their hair is not combed or if they have braids it is long past the time of needing to go back to the beauty shop. You know the needs of your own hair and you can look in a mirror and figure out if you need to wash it, condition it, cut it or get a good wig and cover it. If you have unnatural colors in your hair (blue, pink, bright burgundy, etc.) this is not going to go over well with many employers. My suggestion is, if you like to color your hair, stick with colors that look natural. Extreme hairstyles can be a deterrent for many employers.

MAKEUP

Some women do not wear makeup and they look fresh and beautiful. Most of us need a little help to look fabulous. There is a big difference as to what is considered acceptable makeup for work and what is acceptable makeup for a night out with your husband, boyfriend or the girls. Please be mindful of this difference and do not go loaded down with heavy makeup, glitter or sparkles. I have interviewed many women who wear their makeup in a style that you would see on a video or in a high fashion magazine. Every style has its place so keep it simple when applying for a job.

ACCESSORIES

You can always make an old outfit look and feel new by accessorizing. I love to add a great scarf or vintage jewelry to my outfits. It is an inexpensive way of creating a new look. When you go for an interview, you can always accessorize to make the outfit uniquely you. However, have you ever heard the saying "Less is more"? That is a great motto to accessorize by. You may have a lot of wonderful earrings, bracelets, barouches and rings but do not over do it. Do not wear multiple earrings or big "clunky, chunky" jewelry that jingles when you walk. You do not want your jewelry to dominate your look. And speaking of clunky, chunky and jingling, if you are one of those women that have a key chain filled with everything from baby pictures to mace, you need to leave it at the bottom of your pocket book. There is nothing more irritating than hearing it drop on the receptionist countertop and rattle around the office.

MEN

CLOTHING

I know that many men, particularly young men, live in sweats or jeans and a T-shirt. But it is absolutely unacceptable to show up for an interview dressed like that. It is important that you wear a shirt and tie. This is an essential. When a man walks in my office with a shirt and tie on I know that he is serious about getting a job because he is dressing the part of a professional. If you can take that look one step further and wear a suit, you would easily win points with *anyone* interviewing you. I am confident that anyone in Human Resource feels the same. If you do not have any pants other than jeans, it would be all right. Not ideal… but all right. However, if you do wear jeans you *must* wear the shirt and tie. And by all means, whatever pants you wear make sure that they are not hanging off of your behind. The person interviewing you does not think that you look "cool". They are simply trying to figure out why the pants do not drop to your ankles when you are walking.

If you do not have anything that would be considered to be professional attire, you will need to get something. Whether you borrow it from a family member or friend or go out and purchase something, you need to have at least one good outfit if you are trying to get a job. Now I do understand that you may not have the money to buy something new. If push comes to shove and you do not have anything and cannot borrow something from a friend, roommate or family member, you can always go to a thrift store. Yes, I did say thrift store. There are many businessmen who have enough money to buy new suits, shirts and ties every season and give their suits away to thrift stores or consignment shops. It is not always easy to find a complete suit that may fit you perfectly, but you can always find a good pair of pants and a shirt and tie. I have found many things for my own husband when we were on a budget. I have even found great vintage cufflinks and had my man looking like a million dollars and I only paid a few dollars. The bottom line is this, it does not matter how you get the professional wardrobe…just get it! Dressing professionally for an interview can absolutely make the difference between you getting the job or not getting the job. Having a professional appearance is the first of many criteria of the E-Factor that you will be evaluated on when meeting with an employer.

If you already have a job and are going to fill out an application for another job, whether you are looking for a second job or looking to leave your present job, you must still dress professionally even if you are going to fill out the application on your lunch break or after work. I have interviewed many people who are either in uniforms for other companies or work industrial or construction jobs and come into the office in dirty clothes and worn out uniforms. I know that you may be hard working and your time may be limited but many employers will view your appearance as "sloppy" and not consider you for a position. If there is no other way, based upon your busy work schedule and the hours that a specific company accepts applications, you may have to come straight from work. In that case, if you cannot change your clothes in a restroom, be as clean and pressed as possible. It is important that you tell the receptionist, in addition to the person interviewing you if you do receive an interview that day, that you apologize for not being dressed appropriately but you were only able to fill out the application on your lunch break or after work whichever the case may be. This simple explanation will let the person interviewing you know that you do understand the difference between professional and unprofessional attire and they will not hold it against you in their decision making process.

HAIR

I have seen too many men show up for an interview wearing a baseball cap or a "do-rag". This is *not* professional. Believe me, it *does* count against you. Your hair must be neat and groomed. Keep in mind that some employers do not allow men to wear braids, ponytails or have long hair. So if you fall into this category, they may request that you take out the braids or cut your hair. Every company has its own policies. That includes beards and goatees. Whatever look you are currently wearing, just make sure that it is neat and groomed. If a company wants to hire you, they will inform you of their policies.

ACCESSORIES

If you have any chains, plain or with medallions, I suggest that you do not wear it while you are on the job search. If you do have it on while you are out responding to advertisements for hire, make sure that it is under your shirt.

First impressions are everything. You may never get a second opportunity to change that initial impression, so do not waste the advice of this chapter. Your professional appearance is the first category of your Employability Factor that you are critiqued on and if you fail to impress at this stage, you might as well have stayed home. Even with success in every other category, getting over a poor first impression is an uphill battle when you are competing against countless other applicants for the same position that came in ready for business. Listen to the advice. Make the changes. Get the job.

Professional Appearance
Do's & Don'ts

CLOTHING

- **Do** dress professionally.
- **Do** (men) wear a shirt and tie.
- **Do** wear clothing that covers tattoos.
- **Don't** wear sweats, shorts or jeans.
- **Don't** (women) wear shorts or short skirts.
- **Don't** (women) show your belly button or your cleavage.
- **Don't** (men) wear pants hanging off of your behind.
- **Don't** wear your uniform from another job if it is not clean and pressed.

HAIR & MAKEUP

- **Do** (women) something with your hair. Even if that means slicking it back into a ponytail.
- **Do** (men) be neatly groomed.
- **Don't** wear unnatural colors in your hair (i.e. blue, green, bright burgundy.)
- **Don't** (women) wear a lot of makeup.

ACCESSORIES

- **Do** (women) wear simple jewelry.
- **Don't** (women) wear multiple earrings.
- **Don't** (men) wear any earrings.
- **Don't** wear a tongue ring, lip ring, nose ring, eyebrow piercing or any other facial piercing.
- **Don't** wear sunglasses.
- **Don't** (men) wear baseball caps or "do-rags".
- **Don't** (men) wear heavy chains (plain or with medallions) on the outside of your clothing.
- **Don't** wear too much perfume or cologne.
- **Don't** carry a key chain with a lot of unnecessary items hanging from it.

CHAPTER 2

ETIQUETTE & ATTITUDE

<u>Debbie Fields</u>

Debbie Fields wanted to be in the cookie business all of her life. She loved to bake cookies and believed that people enjoyed eating her creations. At the age of thirteen she began her first entrepreneurial endeavor by selling her cookies to the Oakland A's baseball organization. At the age of twenty she decided to open up her own store and went to various banks with her business plan and carrying a plate of her now famous chocolate chip cookies until she found someone that was willing to offer her a loan to open her first store front cookie shop. By 3:00pm on the grand opening day of her new business she had not sold *one* cookie. Debbie prepared a plate of cookies and went outside and began to give away free samples. That one decision to not give up without a fight and to quickly be creative with a simple marketing strategy turned that one store into over 1000 outlets in 9 countries grossing over $300 million.

Etiquette & Attitude

Now that you know how a professional appearance affects your Employability Factor, let's talk about manners. This is another "make it or break it" category in regards to you being considered for a position with a company. We can all go back in time and hear our mother, father, grandmother or teachers say, "Sit up straight" or "Say please and thank you". Instilling manners is one of the best tools a parent can give a child to succeed in life. This is not boring and old fashion. Being polite is one of the keys that will open up doors in your life. It is expected in a professional setting for you to be polite and customer service oriented. The first indicator of you being able to professionally represent a company in regards to manners is how you act when you are trying to get the job. This starts the moment that you respond to a job opening.

If your first encounter with the company is not in person but over the phone to begin a screening process or simply get directions, make sure that you are in a quiet environment and have pen and paper ready to take down any necessary information. The receptionist does not want to try to talk over screaming babies, loud televisions and car radios. She also does not want to hold on the line while you search for a pen to take down the information. Before you ever get to the Human Resource Manager you have to go through the receptionist. She is the first person that you interact with and the impression that you make, good or bad, will get back to Human Resource Manager. Being polite to the receptionist is one *great* way to receive favor in the selection process. If you win her over with your manners and personality (providing that your appearance is professional) she will usually put your application on top of the stack and possibly include little notes like "Very nice" or "I liked this one".

There is no quicker way of eliminating yourself from getting a job than having an attitude with the receptionist. So remain friendly at all times. Even if the receptionist is a little difficult or moody herself, *she* has a job and *you* are trying to get a job so arguing with her is a losing battle. So how do you win over the receptionist with great manners? Start by saying "Please" and "Thank you" when asking for the application. Be courteous but not too friendly. That means do not lean all over the counter and call her "Girlfriend", "Sweetie" or "Honey". Although I understand many men and woman say this intending to be kind or gracious, but it does not sound professional.

If she asks you any questions do not respond by answering "Yeah", "Uh-huh", "Nah", "Nope". This may be acceptable outside of the workplace, but in a professional setting you should always respond by saying "Yes" or "No". Avoid using any kind of slang language. As your mother may say, "Be on your best behavior". Most of this may sound like common sense, but you would be surprised at how many people eliminate themselves from consideration for a job because of these very reasons. Many times I have corrected someone for using slang or being too familiar, and they are not even aware that they sound unprofessional. I would never select them for a position with my company because good customer service begins with using proper English and having manners.

In addition to the E-Factor of proper professional etiquette that I outlined for conversation, it is equally important that you adhere to the following areas of professional etiquette when filling out an application. The technological age is wonderful. But before you walk into the office, turn off your cell phone and or pager. If you have been using head phones to listen to music on the way to the office, turn off the music and take the headphones completely off of your head (this includes *not* hanging them around your neck). Having applicant's cell phones and pagers going off in the office is disrupting to the receptionist. Remember, she is the first person that you must make a strong impact on so irritating her with all of your pager beeps and cell phone musical songs is not a good idea. And by all means, do not go into the office with a lot of clutter. There is generally limited space in the office to fill out the application and too much clutter makes it cumbersome and crowded for everyone and makes you look unprofessional. This includes bags from shopping, over stuffed book bags, newspapers or food and drink of any kind. A sure way to get eliminated from being considered for a job is showing up with a McDonalds bag and an open can of soda or even popping chewing gum or sucking on a lollypop until your lips and tongue are bright red or blue. Yes, I've seen it all.

Another way people eliminate themselves from consideration for a job is by bringing friends or a spouse into the office. Bringing anyone in with you when you fill out the application or interview can reflect negatively upon you. Even if you have friends that want to apply with the same company, do not go in with friends. You may make a good impression but if your friend acts unprofessionally, it may reflect upon you. If they wanted to hire you, they may not do so because once they hire you, your friend will call incessantly asking why *they* have not been offered a job. If someone does come with you, have them stay in the car or in the lobby of the building or somewhere other than where you are. (This does *not* apply to children. Always leave them at home.)

Bringing children is *never* a good idea. Most employers will not allow children to remain in the office while you fill out the application or interview. Children can be disruptive and distracting to everyone. Also, the employer may assume that if you cannot find a sitter in order to fill out the application, you may also have difficulties with daycare if you are offered a job. Your response to that assumption may legitimately be that you could afford daycare once you get the job. Although I completely understand this logic, most employers will not consider it and you will be eliminated from consideration immediately.

I have also had many applicants who have come in and appear to be bothered, angry or aloof. Depending upon the applicant I may take the time to ask them if everything is all right. I have had applicants respond saying "I am just having a bad day", "I am feeling sick" or "I just found out that my boyfriend is cheating on me" (true story) or any number of reasons as to why they come in the office with what appears to be an attitude. We all have issues in our life. We all have personal struggles and even devastating moments. But when you go to get a job, and even after you get the job, you have to leave it at home and put on that professional smile and handle business. I have been through everything from A to Z and I did not stop wearing makeup, doing my hair or doing my job with a smile on my face. No one would ever know that I was going through difficult situations in my private life. Business is business. You must learn to leave personal challenges at home and walk into the professional setting fresh and ready to work.

What if you do not have any issues in life that may have you walk into an employer's office looking angry or upset. What if you come in as if you are the best possible choice for a position and you would be doing the company a favor if you worked for them. Being confident is one thing. Being a self centered "I am so cute", "I am so smart" or "I am so talented" individual is another. This attitude will get you as far as the front door.

I have also witnessed applicants flirting with each other and exchanging phone numbers. If you are interested in some one you see while you are filling out an application, do *not* pursue it. Trying to get a date is inappropriate while filling out an application. The Human Resource Manager will assume that if you are trying to "hook up" with another applicant while attempting to get the job, you will also be doing the same thing on the job site and this behavior usually causes more problems and conflicts for everyone once the relationship ends.

Lastly, if you show up at the office to fill out an application and the receptionist informs you that you have come on the wrong day or at the wrong time and need to come back, politely say "Thank-you" and return at that particular day and time. I have seen many people get mad and say "I drove all this way for nothing" or "Are you even hiring because I don't want to waste my time". I promise you that even if you do came back on the right day and time you will *not* get the job. No Human Resource Manager is going to hire anyone who has an attitude *before* they get the job. That kind of person would offer no customer service and probably negatively affect the morale of the other employees.

Etiquette & Attitude
Do's & Don'ts

- **Do** call in advance to get the correct day and time as to when the company is taking applications if the advertisement does not specify.
- **Do** be in a quiet environment when calling for information.
- **Do** have pen and paper ready to take down directions or any important information.
- **Do** say "Please" and "Thank-you", "Yes" and "No".
- **Do** be courteous to the receptionist.
- **Do** turn off your pager and cell phone.
- **Don't** say "Yeah", "Uh-huh", "Nah", "Nope".
- **Don't** wear headphones (even around your neck).
- **Don't** talk on your cell phone.
- **Don't** bring children, friends or spouse into the office when filling out the application or when interviewing for a job.
- **Don't** bring clutter (bags, books, groceries, etc.) into the office.
- **Don't** be too familiar (honey, sweetie, girlfriend) with the receptionist.
- **Don't** lean on the receptionist's counter.
- **Don't** use slang.
- **Don't** use profane language.
- **Don't** have an attitude with the receptionist.
- **Don't** bring in food or drinks of any kind.
- **Don't** chew gum or suck on candy.
- **Don't** flirt or exchange telephone numbers with anyone during the application/ interview process.

CHAPTER 3

CREATING A RESUME

<u>Colin Powell</u>

Colin Powell was born in Harlem, New York, the son of a shipping clerk and a seamstress, both of whom were immigrants from Jamaica. Despite the urgings of his parents that he should strive for a good education in order to succeed in life, Powell remained an ordinary student throughout high school. It was not until he joined the ROTC at the City College of New York that he discovered his leadership abilities and went on to be ranked Cadet Colonel which is the highest award at the college. Throughout his military and political career he has done everything from fight in Vietnam to receiving appointments on the National Security Council as well as the Joint Chief of Staff and as Secretary of State. He has arrived at his current position through years of proving himself to be a man of discipline, integrity and determination. Colin Powell had ordinary beginnings. He did not start out with wealth, a private education, or even a clear direction of what he wanted to do with his life. But once he found something (ROTC) that he enjoyed, he gave it everything he had and purposed to be the best. That fortitude and hard work paid off, as he is now a leading world figure both in the military and the political arena. He believes that his life is an example for every young person who they themselves have less than substantial beginnings that if he can succeed...anyone can succeed.

Creating a Resume

For most entry-level positions or service industry positions (retail, waitress, fast food, construction or security, etc.) a resume is not typically required. In fact, I generally never *fully* review a resume that is submitted with an application for an entry-level position. All of the information that I need is requested on the application and is in the format in which I want to use to review your qualifications. However, if there is a resume attached to your application, it does offer you points for professionalism and increase your Employability Factor as I review your application along with the hundreds of other applicants who did not take the time prepare one. If the company that is hiring requires a resume to be submitted, you want to make sure that you have one prepared and ready to offer at a moments notice. Do *not* ask the receptionist or person interviewing you to make a copy of your resume. That crosses the line of professionalism and it will be held against you in the selection process.

I believe that many people do not prepare a resume because they are intimidated by the thought of creating one. What do I say? How do I format it? Where do I start? Let me take the uncertainty out of preparing a resume. Gather the following information:

Step One: Create a list of all of your jobs beginning with the most recent one. Include the name of the company and the city and state in which you worked, your position or title and the time frame in which you were employed (i.e. January 2001-December 2002).

Step Two: For each employer that you have listed, detail your primary responsibilities or professional skills utilized on the job. Use the action verbs that are listed at the end of this chapter to better assist you in personalizing your own work experience.

Step Three: List your educational experience. Everything from high school, college and trade school.

Step Four: Create a list of any awards that you have received or any accomplishments that you have made that you could add to your resume to give your resume personal substance. This may include scholarship recipient, CPR certified, volunteer, ability to speak a foreign language etc.

Once you have gathered this information, it is time to begin your resume. The most popular resume style is a *chronological* format. The chronological resume presents your experience and abilities throughout your job history beginning with the most recent job. If you have serious gaps in your employment history, or if you have little to no employment experience, do not use the chronological format. This format will only accentuate your poor employment record. The format you would want to use is a *functional* resume. This resume style is more flexible and allows you to accentuate your work capabilities instead of your work inconsistencies. This resume style is also great for anyone entering the workforce for the first time or reentering the workforce after a prolonged amount of time due to school, health, or raising a family. No matter what your situation may be, creating a resume, even for first impression's sake, is essential for your E-Factor. Do not put clip art or picture of yourself on the resume. It is not that I would consider it unprofessional, just very corny.

If you have access to the Internet, you can research hundreds of web sites in order to assist you in creating your resume. One of the best is www.microsoft.com/office. If you click on "Templates" on the left hand side of the screen, you will find under the heading "Your Career" sample resumes that you can use. If you do not have access to the Internet at home or at school, you can always go to your local library and utilize a computer free of charge. I have also provided several sample resume formats, chronological and functional, to further assist you. You will of course need some creativity to describe your own work experience and capabilities. To further assist you there is a detailed list of action verbs at the end of this chapter that you can use to describe your job duties and accomplishments. Do not be intimidated…you can do this!

Creating a Resume
Do's & Don'ts

- **Do** take the time to create a resume.
- **Do** make plenty of copies for your job search.
- **Don't** ask the receptionist or person interviewing you to make a copy of your resume.
- **Don't** put clip art on your resume.
- **Don't** include a picture of yourself (unless requested by the company).

Chronological Resume Example

Your Name	Phone Number
Street Address, City State Zip Code	E-mail address

Professional Profile

Briefly describe you professional background and education relevant to this position.

• Relevant Skill • Relevant Skill • Relevant Skill • Relevant Skill	• Relevant Skill • Relevant Skill • Relevant Skill • Relevant Skill

Professional Experience

Company Name, City, State

Dates of Employment

Your Title

Achievements:
- Achievement
- Achievement
- Achievement

Responsibilities:
- Job Responsibility
- Job Responsibility
- Job Responsibility

Company Name, City, State

Dates of Employment

Your Title

Achievements:
- Achievement
- Achievement
- Achievement

Responsibilities:
- Job Responsibility
- Job Responsibility
- Job Responsibility

Education

College, University or Trade School, City, State

Degree Obtained

Date Graduated

References

References are available upon request.

Chronological Resume Example

Your Name

Street Address, City, State, Zip Code Phone Number E-mail Address

<u>Objective</u>	Describe you career goal or idea
<u>Experience</u>	Job Title
	Dates of Employment, Company Name, City, State
	▪ Job Responsibility / Achievement
	▪ Job Responsibility / Achievement
	▪ Job Responsibility / Achievement
	Job Title
	Dates of Employment, Company Name, City, State
	▪ Job Responsibility / Achievement
	▪ Job Responsibility / Achievement
	▪ Job Responsibility / Achievement
	Job Title
	Dates of Employment, Company Name, City, State
	▪ Job Responsibility / Achievement
	▪ Job Responsibility / Achievement
	▪ Job Responsibility / Achievement
	Job Title
	Dates of Employment, Company Name, City, State
	▪ Job Responsibility / Achievement
	▪ Job Responsibility / Achievement
	▪ Job Responsibility / Achievement
<u>Education</u>	School Name, City, State
	▪ Degree Obtained
	▪ Special Awards / Accomplishments
<u>Interests</u>	Briefly describe interests that may pertain to the job you want.
<u>References</u>	References are available on request.

Functional Resume Example

Your Name	
Street Address	
City, State, Zip Code	
Phone Number	
E-mail Address	

<u>Objective</u>

Briefly describe your career goal.

<u>Professional Profile</u>

Field or Area of Accomplishment

- Achievement
- Achievement
- Achievement

Field or Area of Accomplishment

- Achievement
- Achievement
- Achievement

Field or Area of Accomplishment

- Achievement
- Achievement
- Achievement

Field or Area of Accomplishment

- Achievement
- Achievement
- Achievement

Field or Area of Accomplishment

- Achievement
- Achievement
- Achievement

<u>Work History</u>

Dates of Employment, Job Title, Company Name, City, State
Dates of Employment, Job Title, Company Name, City, State
Dates of Employment, Job Title, Company Name, City, State
Dates of Employment, Job Title, Company Name, City, State

<u>Education</u>

Dates of Attendance, School Name, City, State

- Degree Obtained
- Special Award / Accomplishment

<u>References</u>

References are available on request.

Management	Communication	Research	Technical	Teaching
achieved	addressed	clarified	analyzed	adapted
administered	arbitrated	collected	assembled	advised
analyzed	arranged	conceived	built	clarified
assigned	authored	critiqued	calculated	coached
attained	communicated	detected	computed	communicated
chaired	corresponded	diagnosed	designed	coordinated
conceived	counseled	disproved	devised	defined
contracted	developed	evaluated	engineered	developed
consolidated	defined	examined	fabricated	enabled
coordinated	directed	extracted	inspected	encouraged
decided	drafted	identified	maintained	evaluated
delegated	edited	inspected	operated	explained
developed	enlisted	interpreted	overhauled	facilitated
directed	formulated	interviewed	programmed	guided
encouraged	influenced	investigated	remodeled	informed
evaluated	interpreted	organized	repaired	initiated
executed	lectured	researched	solved	instructed
handled	mediated	reported	trained	lectured
implemented	moderated	reviewed	upgraded	persuaded
improved	motivated	searched		presented
incorporated	negotiated	studied		set goals
increased	persuaded	summarized		stimulated
inspired	promoted	surveyed		taught
launched	publicized	systematized		trained
led	reconciled	wrote		updated
managed	reunited			
motivated	renegotiated			
organized	reported			
outlined	researched			
oversaw	summarized			
planned	spoke			
prioritized	translated			
produced	wrote			
recommended				
reevaluated				
rejected				
reported				
reviewed				
scheduled				
strengthened				
supervised				
united				

Financial	Creative	Helping	Clerical or Detail
adjusted	acted	advised	activated
administered	applied	aided	altered
allocated	composed	assessed	assembled
analyzed	conceived	assisted	approved
appraised	conceptualized	brought	arranged
audited	created	clarified	catalogued
balanced	designed	coached	classified
budgeted	developed	coordinated	collected
calculated	directed	counseled	compiled
compared	established	dealt	described
computed	evaluated	demonstrated	dispatched
developed	fashioned	diagnosed	edited
estimated	formed	educated	estimated
forecast	formulated	encouraged	executed
forecasted	founded	enlisted	gathered
managed	illustrated	expedited	generated
marketed	instituted	facilitated	implemented
planned	integrated	familiarized	inspected
projected	introduced	guided	listed
reevaluated	invented	helped	maintained
reconciled	loaded	inspired	monitored
researched	molded	maintained	observed
sold	originated	modified	operated
	perceived	performed	organized
	performed	referred	overhauled
	planned	rehabilitated	prepared
	presented	represented	processed
	produced	supported	proofread
	refined	upheld	published
	rewrote		purchased
	updated		recorded
			reduced
			retrieved
			screened
			specified
			streamlined
			systematized

Additional Action Verbs

anticipated	experimented	lectured	received	scheduled
arbitrated	explained	lifted	recommended	selected
ascertained	expressed	listened	reconciled	sensed
charted	extracted	logged	painted	separated
checked	filed	maintained	perceived	served
classified	financed	made	performed	sewed
collected	fixed	managed	persuaded	shaped
completed	followed	manipulated	photographed	shared
conducted	formulated	mediated	piloted	showed
conserved	founded	memorized	planned	sketched
consolidated	gathered	modeled	played	solved
constructed	gave	monitored	predicted	sorted
controlled	generated	motivated	prepared	summarized
coordinated	guided	navigated	prescribed	supervised
counseled	handled	negotiated	presented	supplied
created	headed	observed	printed	symbolized
decided	helped	obtained	processed	synergized
defined	hypothesized	offered	produced	synthesized
delivered	identified	operated	programmed	systematized
detailed	illustrated	ordered	projected	talked
detected	imagined	organized	promoted	taught
determined	implemented	originated	proof-read	tended
devised	improved	painted	protected	tested
diagnosed	improvised	perceived	provided	trained
directed	increased	performed	publicized	transcribed
discovered	influenced	persuaded	purchased	translated
dispensed	informed	photographed	recorded	traveled
displayed	initiated	piloted	recruited	treated
disproved	innovated	planned	reduced	troubleshot
dissected	inspected	played	referred	tutored
distributed	installed	predicted	rehabilitated	typed
diverted	instituted	prepared	related	unified
dramatized	instructed	prescribed	rendered	united
drew	integrated	presented	repaired	upgraded
drove	interpreted	printed	reported	used
eliminated	interviewed	processed	represented	utilized
empathized	invented	produced	researched	verbalized
enforced	inventoried	programmed	resolved	warned
established	investigated	questioned	responded	washed
estimated	judged	raised	restored	weighed
evaluated	kept	read	retrieved	wired
examined	led	realized	reviewed	worked
expanded	learned	reasoned	risked	

CHAPTER 4

FILLING OUT THE APPLICATION

<u>Alonzo Herndon</u>

Alonzo Herndon was born a slave in Georgia in 1858. He received only one year of formal education, but learned barbering and opened his first barbershop at the age of twenty. He eventually owned and operated three barbershops. One of them, The Crystal Palace, was considered the most elegant in the country. It was decorated with crystal chandeliers and marble floors that spanned one full city block in downtown Atlanta. He invested his barbering income in real estate, becoming by the early 1900's the wealthiest African-American property owner in Atlanta. His most significant and lasting business venture began when he acquired what would become the Atlanta Life Insurance Company. The Atlanta Life Insurance Company is the largest African-American owned stockholder insurance company in America today. Alonzo Herndon died at the age of 69 leaving behind a legacy of success. A success made sweeter having starting out his life as a slave.

Filling out the Application

Every employer has different prerequisites and information that they may request during the application process. This may include a language skills test, writing a short essay on one of their company's core values, or writing a short essay on yourself and your abilities. But there is some basic information that all employers are going to request on their application that you will need to provide. Your Employability Factor is measured by how completely and accurately you fill out the requested information. Because of this, you should always be well prepared when filling out the application. There is nothing worse than having someone ask the receptionist for a phone book to get past employment information or leaving areas blank because they cannot remember the information that is being requested. Do not leave home without all of the necessary information. That means that you should have it written down on a "cheat sheet" prior to coming in to fill out the application so that you present yourself as organized and professional. I have provided that "cheat sheet" at the end of this chapter. I also recommend that you bring your own ink pen (preferably black) and a pocket dictionary to avoid misspelled words on your application. (Do not use the dictionary if there is a language test that you must take, as this would be considered cheating.)

When going to fill out an application, confirm the hours that the company is accepting applications and arrive as early as possible during those hours. If you show up late in the day when the office starts to get busy, you may be lost in the crowd. The Human Resource Manager will usually spend more time with an applicant if they do not have a room full of other people waiting to be interviewed. If you do not have the liberty to come in *anytime* during specific hours but you have to set an appointment, make sure that you are at least fifteen minutes early.

The following is a detailed list of what you will be asked to provide on your application:

PERSONAL INFORMATION

One of the most important pieces of information that will be required on the application is a current telephone number. This is typically expected to be your home phone number but I have found a recent trend that most applicants put their cell phone number as their contact number. This is perfectly acceptable. The reason why a reliable telephone number is so important is because the Human Resource Manager will disregard your application if they attempt to contact you with a job offer and cannot reach you. With that in mind, if your telephone has been or is on the verge of being disconnected, do not leave it as a contact number. It is not ideal but I do understand that you may have to leave your next-door neighbor, cousins or grandmother's telephone number as your contact number. If you have to use someone else's number, do not tell the person taking the application that it is not *your* number because you may be perceived as being unstable. Make sure that you can trust the person whose telephone number you are using will give you the message the same day if they receive a call from the company with a job offer or request for a second interview.

You also need your current address and your previous address. This includes the city, state and zip code. In addition to this, you should also bring your driver's license or state identification and social security card or birth certificate as well as proof of proper work authorization if necessary.

EMPLOYMENT HISTORY

This is usually the most critical part of the application because it tells a lot about your job stability and work ethic. You will need to bring a detailed listing of your previous employers. Never put in this section "See Resume". Your resume may have some of the information required but not all. This list should include the following: the name of the company; complete address; telephone number; immediate supervisor's name; a description of your job duties; the date that you were hired and the date that you left *and* the reason for leaving that company. If you have worked for a number of different employers and have only stayed for a few months with each employer, you do not look like a stable person. It costs time and money for an employer to hire you. Most employers pay for criminal background checks, employment and educational history verifications, drug tests, uniforms and training. No employer wants to make an investment into someone that may only stay with their company for a short period of time. They are looking for longevity. An application that shows that you have only worked two months here and six months there makes you look like a waste of time and money.

This portion of the application allows an employer to look at your work history at a glance. It takes a moment for an employer to look at the dates of your employment and the reason why *you* say you left the company to make a quick determination if it is worth considering you for a position. If your work history is poor, do not lie to make it look better. Most employers do some sort of employment history verification on your dates of employment and they will find out if you falsify the information.

What if you fall into the category of having a poor work history because you have only worked summer jobs while going to school or have been an at home wife and mother? Every employer is going to view this differently and may have biases beyond your control. I suggest that you convince them that although you have little to no *formal* work experience, you do posses the qualities that an employer is looking for – punctuality, customer service oriented, works well as a team, ability to multitask, set schedules and follow routines, work faithfully without constant supervision, manage people (children or fellow students during a team project fall under this category).

As an employer, a student that has no formal work experience can convince me to offer them a position if they can explain that they are committed to their studies and achieving excellence, that they have good grades as a result of being to class on time, taking notes and adhering to a strict study schedule and would bring that same commitment to the workplace. That they have study groups with people of various personalities and can get along well with everyone. Convince the employer that you know what qualities they are looking for when hiring a solid employee and that you possess those qualities but you have simply used those for academic pursuits and now would like to use them in the workplace.

As an at home wife and mother, you should do the same thing. Convince the Human Resource Manager that you possess all of the qualities that an employer is looking for, but you have simply used those qualities in your home and now would like to use them in the workplace. Anyone that can get children fed, dressed, hair done, pack lunches, confirm homework assignments are complete *and* in the book bag, keep a clean house, run errands, fix dinner while washing the clothes *and* helping with homework and a million things in between and all of this in only *one* day in my opinion would make a *great* employee. You simply need to learn how to explain your abilities in a manner in which an employer can understand how it would transfer into the workplace.

If you fall into the category of having a poor work history, the best thing to do is acknowledge this in the interview. Let the Human Resource Manager know that you are aware that you do not look like a solid employee on paper. But you have matured, corrected some personal obstacles, found reliable day care, are no longer dependant on public transportation or whatever the case may be and are now hoping that a door may be open to you so that you may prove yourself as a valuable asset to their company. I have hired many people based upon this very scenario. Some I have given the opportunity to prove themselves and they have been very successful. Others continue in their old pattern and within a matter of a short time are terminated or quit.

Even if your current job is not giving you enough hours or the money that you would like to receive, having a low paying job with few hours is better than having no job at all. It is a foolish choice to quit a job with absolutely nothing lined up. It is also foolish to quit a job and not give a two-week notice. You never know what circumstances may come in your life and you may need to return to a former employer for a full-time or part-time job. If you did not leave that employer in good standing, you will not be eligible for re-hire. This also makes you look unstable and unreliable. In the section where the employer asks you to state the reason why you left your previous employers, I have had applicants put statements like "Didn't like the people", "Too much work", "Fired", "Car broke down", "Unfair treatment" or "Looking for better opportunities" and yet they have not worked for six months to a year. Do not state something, although it may be true, that would make a prospective employer think twice about your work ethic, your attitude, your stability and your ability to commit to the job. Even if you were fired, the reason for leaving that you put on the application should always be stated as if it were a positive move for you or something beyond you control such as "Given a better job offer with opportunities for advancement", "The company downsized my department", "Laid off" or at the very least "I relocated and the job was too far of a distance to travel".

Also, when responding to employment verifications the only information that a past employer can offer a prospective employer is the dates that you worked for the company, your position and pay rate. They cannot, by law, state "We fired him for sleeping" or "I wouldn't hire her because she always comes in late". That does not mean that some employers do not do just that, but most give only the information they are legally able to give. I am not telling you this to give you license to do *whatever* you want to and leave a company *however* you want to but I am telling you this so that if in your past you have been fired, the company that you are interviewing with should not hear any of those details.

PERSONAL REFERANCES

For this section you will need at least three people that a potential employer may contact that would say that you are a reliable, responsible and hardworking person. You need to have their name, telephone number, address, occupation and the number of years that you have known them. It cannot be a family member. You may list a pastor, teacher, coach, former supervisor, etc. Always ask the person that you would like to use as a reference if it is all right with them if you do so. The employer may be calling that person and you do not want him or her to be upset with you for using their personal information on an application. Make sure that your reference knows your full legal name. That means if your full legal name is Daniel Michael Turner and everyone calls you Mickey Turner, confirm that your references have this information. If they only know you by your nick name they may tell the employer confirming the reference as Daniel Turner that they do not know who you are which could affect your opportunity for selection.

SPECIAL ACADEMIC AND/OR PROFESSIONAL
ACCOMPLISHMENTS & AWARDS

In this area you may list awards and or accomplishments in your life such as Scholarship recipient, R.O.T.C., Habitat for Humanity volunteer, Church volunteer, CPR certified, Boy or Girl Scout, Student Council Member, Dean's List, Honor Society, Fraternity or Sorority member. It is important to have accomplishments on your application. It shows a level of responsibility, commitment and depth that employers are looking for.

WORK AVAILABILITY

Every employer has different shift availability. What they have available is totally dependant on the company itself and the service they provide. Some companies are open Monday thru Friday from 9:00am to 5:00pm. While others are open twenty-four hours a day, seven days a week. Most people want to work Monday thru Friday on the first shift. If that is what you want and the company that you are filling out the application for is hiring for that shift...great! But many employers are open seven days a week and are hiring for shifts in the morning, afternoon and evening. If that is the case, you need to be as flexible as possible when filling out the section for your work availability. It is acceptable for you to list the days and shifts that you would *prefer* to work in addition to listing the days and shifts that you would be *able* to work. The more flexible you are the better your opportunities will be in getting a job. If you have limited availability, it will probably limit your chances for selection. Employers interview many applicants' daily and usually only have a few positions available. The more flexible you are will definitely increase your chances of selection.

I have many applicants that say they can only work Monday thru Friday on the first shift. If you say that is all that you are able to work, 99% of the time employers are not able to offer you a job if their company is large and is hiring for more than one shift. Not because you are unqualified but because if a day shift becomes available, the people that are already working for the company usually receive the opportunity to transfer into that shift before they would hire someone new to fill that particular opening. If you are not hired based upon the days and shift that you stated that you are able to work and you call the company a month or more later and want to change your availability, it still may not help your chances of being selected. Since the time that you came into their office to fill out the application they have probably met with a few hundred other people and your application has long since been filed away. Flexibility equals opportunity.

EXPECTED PAY RATE

You can eliminate yourself from a position strictly based upon the pay rate that you note on the application that you expect to receive. Most companies have a particular start rate for every position. If you state that you expect to receive $12 an hour and the position starts at $10 an hour, you will not be considered for the position. I do understand that you have bills to pay and you may have determined that you need a specific dollar amount hourly in order for you to meet your financial obligations. The reality is that you may have to take a lower paying job and work overtime or even work one full time job along with a part time job to make ends meet. I know this is not the ideal situation. I have interviewed many people who ask for more money than I can offer and say it is because of bills, or "That's what I made on my last job", or "I know that I have the experience to get paid more money". All of this may be true, but every position has a set pay rate and you will eliminate yourself from consideration if you are determined to receive more than a company can offer. I have had people call me back anywhere from one to three months later and say "I'll take anything…I just need a job". They wasted all that time having *no* money at all coming in rather than taking one step backwards to take two steps forward.

Remember, you are one of many applicants that the Human Resource Manager interviews. You are not the only choice for the job. The best response to the question of "What pay rate do you expect to receive" would be to answer "Flexible", "Negotiable" or "Open". This gives you the opportunity to discuss pay rates without eliminating yourself from consideration because you request too much. Many people believe that if they say they will work for $8 an hour then that is what they will receive even if the position pays $12 an hour. That is not true. No reputable company will give you less than the regular starting pay rate. Applicants always win me over when they say that they are willing to work for whatever the starting rate is with the confidence that as long as they can get in the door their work ethic will open up opportunities for economic advancement.

EDUCATION

This section would include High School diploma or GED, College, Business or Trade school. You should bring a complete list of the schools you have attended beginning with high school. Include the name and address. Most employers require a minimum of a High School diploma or GED. Many employers require that you provide proof of having obtained it by showing the employer the original copy. So keep it in a safe place. If you do not have a High School diploma or GED and falsify your application, because many employers today conduct an educational background investigation, you will get caught for falsifying your application and subsequently be terminated. My suggestion is, if you do not have a High School diploma or GED equivalent, you need to take the time to get it. Not having this will only limit your opportunities. I also suggest that you acquire some basic computer skills. I do understand the challenge of not having the resources to pay for continued education classes but you would be surprised what is available free of charge. It just takes time, determination, some phone calls and patience. I would begin by contacting the various workforce development agencies in your city. You can also contact your local libraries and churches. There is always some agency that is willing to offer you assistance. You just have to take the time to seek them out.

MILITARY BACKGROUND

Most employers will ask if you have ever served in the military and consider your performance in the military the same way they would consider your performance and good standing with any other previous employer. Many employers will not hire you if you have a dishonorable discharge. Every company has its own policy regarding military discharge requirements. If you have been in the military, bring a copy of your DD214 with you because the person interviewing you may request to review it. If you are considering going into military, please know that your behavior during your tour of duty will remain with you long after you leave. Everything is documented and it could potentially affect you in the future when seeking employment if you do not leave the military in good standing.

CRIMINAL BACKGOUND

Most employers will ask you if you have ever been convicted of a criminal offense that has not been annulled or sealed by the court. Anything that you may have been convicted of as a juvenile will not appear on your record and you do not have to divulge this information. However, anything that you were charged with as an adult will appear. Every employer has a different policy regarding criminal history. Please know that your criminal record is not like your credit report. Nothing drops off after seven years. Answer the information honestly. If you lie, you will probably get caught because most employers do some kind of criminal background investigation searching seven to ten years back. If you are honest, they may be able to work with you depending upon the charge. If you lie and they do the investigation and find out that you have a criminal conviction that you did not divulge on the application you will be terminated once that information is received for falsifying your application.

Many employers cannot hire you if you have a felony of any kind or a misdemeanor that falls under the category of drugs, theft or violence. I have seen many applicants that I would hire if they did not have a criminal background record. No matter how much I like the person or how long ago they were convicted, regulations regarding the company policy is the only thing that matters. Consider this, jumping the turnstile at a train station is considered "Theft of services" and is a misdemeanor charge. Think about it… for not paying a dollar and some change they now have a theft charge on their criminal background record that disqualifies them from applying with a great number of employers. I also see a lot of what I call "Waiting to exhale" charges. These are the property vandalism, physical violence, terrorist phone call threats that usually occur after a bitter breakup. The consequences of the foolish choices that we make affect us in ways that we can never anticipate. And usually last longer than we could ever imagine.

DRUG TESTING

Many employers ask on the application if you would be able to pass a drug test. Yes, employers do drug test. In fact over eighty percent of all employers drug test. Most employers drug test prior to you receiving the job and many do random drug tests after you get the job. Drugs, especially marijuana, stay in the system for a very long time and will be detected in the urine. Drug test labs know all of the tricks of those who know that they will fail the drug test and therefore attempt to alter their urine sample. It does not work. They have seen it all and I have heard it all! All of the excuses about "I ate a salad with poppy seeds" or "My roommate smokes but I don't" are not going to help your case. Once you fail, you are out of a job. If you use drugs you are then saying that getting high is more important than supporting your family, having a roof over your head, paying your bills, caring for your children, paying for college, and all of the other day to day needs that having a steady income provides for. I have had many people lose their job for this very reason. Again, life is about choices. My suggestion is to enjoy your life in your right mind.

As you can see, because of the extensive information that employers will expect you to provide on the application, it is imperative that you come prepared. All of this may seem overwhelming and maybe even a little tedious. I can guarantee you that filling out an application fully and properly is one of the basic E-Factor requirements in being considered for a job. Review the information that I have detailed in this chapter and begin making, if you do not already have it prepared, a "cheat sheet" that includes all of your personal information that you now know an employer will request. Creating a "cheat sheet" will make the application process much easier for you in addition to making it easier for the Human Resource Manager to review your information and consider you for a position.

If you do not hear from an employer within a week, it is acceptable for you to call and check on the status of your application unless they specifically told you not to do so. You will probably get the Human Resource Manager or Assistant Manager's voice mail. Be very specific and be polite State your name, the date that you filled out the application and your return telephone number. You can also state that you hope he or she finds you qualified for a position because you would appreciate the opportunity to work for their company. If you do not get a return phone call, call the office again a week later and leave another message. Be polite and professional. I get a lot of messages where the applicant says with an aggressive tone "You *never* called me and I *know* that you are hiring because I see your ad in the paper so look at my application and call me back"! Once you cross the line of sincere interest and move into being pushy, you will *never* get the job. To be honest, if you have not received a call within three weeks, there will probably *not* be a job offer given to you. Remember, there are only a few positions available to every hundred applications submitted and what you need concerning shift, days off and pay rate they may not have available even if they liked you. So put in applications with as many employers as you can while following the Employability Factor instructions in this book and a door *will* be opened to you.

Filling out the Application
Do's & Don'ts

- **Do** bring a resume.
- **Do** arrive early before it gets too busy and you get lost in the crowd.
- **Do** arrive at least fifteen minutes early if you have a scheduled time to fill out the application.
- **Do** bring your own pen (preferably with black ink).
- **Do** bring a pocket dictionary to assist you in writing an essay if the application requires one.
- **Do** write legibly.
- **Do** bring a detailed list of personal information (complete present address, previous address, telephone number,)
- **Do** bring your driver's license or state identification and social security card or birth certificate as well as proof of proper work authorization if necessary.
- **Do** bring a detailed account of your previous jobs (name of the company, address, telephone number, supervisor's name, dates of employment, amount of pay that you received when you started, amount of pay that you received when you left and a detailed account of your job duties.)
- **Do** bring a list of three references (name, address, telephone number, number of years that you have known the person). The references must be a non-family member (teacher, former employer, pastor etc.)
- **Do** bring educational information. This would include the name and address of any school that you may have attended beginning with High School.
- **Do** bring a copy of any certificate that you may have including your High School Diploma or GED.
- **Do** bring your DD214 if you have served in the military.
- **Do** be flexible in the shifts and the days of the week that you are able to work.
- **Do** be honest with all criminal background information.
- **Don't** ask for a phone book to help you fill out the application
- **Don't** (if at all possible) limit yourself on your work availability (shift and days).
- **Don't** ask for more money than the position offers.
- **Don't** put negative reasons as to why you left your previous employers.
- **Don't** leave an employer without giving a two-week notice.
- **Don't** do anything foolish to get a criminal record.
- **Don't** lie about your criminal or educational information.
- **Don't** use drugs.
- **Don't** call everyday to check the status of your application.
- **Don't** leave any "pushy" messages while checking on the status of your application.

YOUR PERSONALIZED CHEAT SHEET

PERSONAL INFORMATION

Present Address: _____

Previous Address: _____

Current Telephone Number: _____

Alternate Contact Number: _____

EMPLOYMENT HISTORY

Name of the Company: _____

Address: _____

Telephone Number: _____

Supervisors Name: _____

Dates of Employment: _____

Reason for Leaving: _____

Job Duties/Accomplishments: _____

_____

_____

Name of the Company: _____

Address: _____

Telephone Number: _____

Supervisors Name: _____

Dates of Employment: _____

Reason for Leaving: _____

Job Duties/Accomplishments: _____

_____

_____

Name of the Company: _____

Address: _____

Telephone Number: _____

Supervisors Name: _____

Dates of Employment: _____

Reason for Leaving: _____

Job Duties/Accomplishments: _____

_____

Name of the Company: _____

Address: _____

Telephone Number: _____

Supervisors Name: _____

Dates of Employment: _____

Reason for Leaving: _____

Job Duties/Accomplishments: _____

_____

PERSONAL REFERANCES

Name: _____

Address: _____

Telephone Number: _____

Number of years that you have known this person: _____

Name: _____

Address: _____

Telephone Number: _____

Number of years that you have known this person: _____

Name: _____

Address: _____

Telephone Number: _____

Number of years that you have known this person: _____

SPECIAL ACADEMIC AND/OR PROFESSIONAL
ACCOMPLISHMENTS & AWARDS

_____

_____

_____

EDUCATION

Name of the School: _____

Address: _____

Degree or Field of Study: _____

Name of the School: _____

Address: _____

Degree or Field of Study: _____

CHAPTER 5

THE INTERVIEW

Oprah Winfrey

Born in a small farming town in Mississippi, Oprah's early life offered no glimpse of the extraordinary accomplishments that were to come from this ordinary child that was shuffled between parents and grandparents. She had a troubled adolescence plagued with poverty and sexual abuse but at the age of 16 found her direction in life when she won a partial scholarship to Tennessee State University after entering a public speaking contest. With her genuine warm and personable style and charismatic presence she parlayed that opportunity and moved her way up in broadcasting from radio newscaster, news anchor to morning talk show host. She launched the *Oprah Winfrey Show* in 1986 as a nationally syndicated program. The show grossed $125 million by the end of its first year, of which Winfrey received $30 million. Oprah says of herself "I don't think of myself as a poor, deprived ghetto girl who made it rich. I think of myself as somebody who from an early age knew I was responsible for myself, and that I had to work hard and be good at what I did to be successful."

The Interview

Throughout this book you have been given practical instruction on your appearance, etiquette and attitude, resume writing and filling out the application. These are the initial categories of the Employability Factor that you will be critiqued on during the selection process. I will be operating under the assumption that you have listened to my advice and have come in on time, dressed professionally, having manners with a resume in hand and having filled out your application fully and properly. It is now the moment of truth. You must meet with the Human Resource Manager. I will be using myself as an example throughout this chapter as the person that will be interviewing you and, for a very brief moment, put you under a microscope as I determine if you are the right candidate to be selected for a position. The scrutiny begins the moment that I take your application and call your name to come back to my office.

While you are waiting to be interviewed, it is imperative that you are prepared to have your name called at any moment. An applicant can eliminate themselves from consideration strictly based upon how they act or what they do while waiting to be interviewed. When I call someone's name, I do not want to look up and see them slouched in a chair, eating or drinking, reading a newspaper, talking on a cell phone, or anything else other than waiting to be interviewed. If you brought anything with you, you should have yourself organized and ready to greet me the moment I call your name. When I call your name, it is best if you respond by saying "Yes" then stand and be prepared to shake my hand. Do not grip my hand too hard or too soft. Give me a firm handshake with your *right* hand. Never shake with your left hand unless you have a medical reason as to why you cannot use your right hand. At this point, I will escort you back to my office and I will review your application and resume and ask you all the questions necessary to determine if you are right for the company. Your response to my questions will be critical in my decision to consider you for a position. The interview is the final category for critiquing your overall E-Factor.

It is important while in the interview that you follow a few tips that may seem minor but can have a big impact on how you are perceived beginning with your posture. To give off the best body language impression, do not lean all the way back in the chair. Sitting up straight with your back not touching the back of the chair makes you appear the best. Women, it looks better if you sit with both feet touching the floor while crossing your feet at the ankles rather than crossing your legs at the knee. Men, you usually take up more room in the chair as opposed to the ladies so your back will probably touch the back of the chair. There is no problem with that, just do not slouch or sit with your legs spread as wide as the chair. The best thing that you can do is place a chair in front of a mirror and look at how you are sitting so you can see exactly what I will be seeing when you sit in my office. Body language is an important visual impression in the decision making process of the Human Resource Manager. So please pay attention to how you are sitting. Give direct eye contact. Not giving a person eye contact when they are talking to you gives the perception that you are timid, aloof, not being truthful, lazy or just plain crazy. So sit up straight, look me in the eyes and do *not* eat the candy. Don't eat the candy? Yes, many professionals have a candy jar on their desk for themselves and to share with the office staff. I worked with a woman that kept chocolates in a jar on her desk because that was her manager's favorite candy and providing chocolates was a sure way of getting him to come into her office so she could discuss pressing issues of the day without having to wait in line behind every other person in the office who needed a little "face time". Human Resource Managers may interview up to one hundred applicants per week. They certainly do not want to accommodate the sweet tooth of everyone that enters their office. Asking for a piece of candy may seem trivial but it breaks the professional standard of an interview.

The following are some of the questions that you may be asked during the interview. It is important for you to be prepared with a response. Review the possible questions that you may be asked and practice a brief response. This will help you to be confident in the interview.

1. Tell me about yourself?

Give a brief description of your education or specialized training, skills, work history, work ethic etc. Highlight anything that would make you an asset to the company and ideal for the position. Do not use this opportunity to discuss personal tragedies or current difficulties that you may be facing. Although I do understand that many people who I interview may feel pressed on every side because they do not have a job, many Human Resource Managers do *not* want to hear that you are struggling. You have no idea of what *their* life experience may be. If they have never struggled in their life to pay bills, raise children, get around on public transportation, be homeless, care for a sick family member or whatever the case may be, they may perceive your "challenges" as instability or a future liability to the company as you may not stay with them for very long because another situation may come up that could affect your employment. So keep it positive and be specific.

_____

_____

_____

_____

_____

2. What are your personal strengths?

Always give attributes that a potential employer would view as an asset to their company. Example: punctuality, ability to work well with others, computer literate, customer service oriented, self-starter, highly motivated, etc.

_____

_____

_____

_____

_____

3. What are your areas of improvement?

You do not want to reveal anything that may eliminate you from a job. Anything that you list as an area of improvement, follow up with a brief description of what steps you are proactively taking to improve in that particular area. For example, you may not be computer literate. Do not say that you do not know anything about computers. You should say something like "I do not have as much computer experience as I would like…however I am presently taking classes (or have enrolled/will be enrolling) to gain more knowledge and become more proficient". We all have areas of improvement. Even the CEO's of major companies have areas of improvement. Be it personal or professional. It is important that you identify an area and present steps that you are taking or will be taking to improve.

_____
_____
_____
_____
_____

3. What are your goals for the future?

Your response may be something like "Advance within the company", "Return to college part-time", "Own your own business", etc. Make sure that your response does not eliminate you from consideration. For example, do not say that you are hoping to relocate in a few months to another state to go to school or move closer to family. No company will invest their time and money into selecting and training you if they are unsure of your longevity.

_____
_____
_____
_____
_____

4. Recount a situation with a previous employer where you had to assist a difficult or angry customer?

Great customer service skills are a requirement for almost any position in any company. Recount a situation in which you were friendly, helpful and calm. Do not describe the person that you were assisting as "crazy" or "stupid". You should describe the customer's complaint and explain how you assisted in resolving the problem swiftly and professionally while keeping the customer satisfied with the company.

_____
_____
_____
_____
_____

5. What is one of your greatest accomplishments (personal or professional)?

Example: Becoming a supervisor/manager at your previous job, completing college, volunteering with a specific organization, receiving an academic or athletic scholarship, etc.

_____

_____

_____

_____

_____

6. What did you like *most* about your previous job?

Do not say that what you liked the most was that you did not have to do that much work. Or do not say that you did not like *anything*. You are being critiqued on your response. So be professional. You can respond by saying, " You enjoyed the challenge of the cross-training program that the company offered", "You enjoyed assisting customers resolve their problems with a product", "You enjoyed the teamwork that you experienced with your fellow co-workers" or "You enjoyed putting your education to practical use".

_____

_____

_____

_____

_____

7. What did you like *least* about your previous job?

Do not take this opportunity to go into a list of complaints that you may have about your previous employer. If you complain in the interview about your previous employer, I can guarantee that you will *not* get the job. Although your complaints may be legitimate, it makes you sound like a negative and disgruntled person who may be a thorn in their side if they hire you. So respond to that question by saying something like "I really enjoyed my previous job. But if I had to choose a job duty that was my least favorite it would be"…writing reports, taking out the garbage, sweeping the floor, late night inventory or whatever your least favorite duty was. But add to that statement that you did it without complaint because you understood that everyone has a role to play in making the work place run effectively and efficiently. Does that sound phony? Well it probably is. We all have job duties that we do not enjoy. Remember, you are trying to get a job and complaining about a job duty, no matter how menial, does not help you look professional or worth taking a chance to offer you a job that will also, like your previous employer, probably include a few undesirable responsibilities.

_____

_____

_____

_____

_____

Once you leave my office, I will then rate your overall Employability Factor. Based upon a combination of your appearance, etiquette and attitude, information obtained from the application and professionalism in the interview, I can then make the determination as to what file to place your application. I have three categories that range from "NO", "MAYBE" and "YES". There are a number of reasons as to why you would fall into a specific category. It may be one reason or a combination of many. The following is a brief description of the E-Factor reasoning that I and many other employers have as to why we select one person over another.

<u>NO:</u> I would *not* offer you a position with the company.

- You are unprofessional in your appearance, etiquette and attitude.
- You have a conviction on your criminal background record that violates the company policy.
- You do not have a High School Diploma or GED.
- You have a Dishonorable or "Other Than Honorable" discharge from the military.
- You have a poor work history. Or if you have been a student or at home wife and mother you did not convince me that you have the qualities that an employer is looking for and that you can commit to the structure of the workplace.
- You did not fully complete the application.
- You have no flexibility in the shifts and/or days you are able to work.
- Your excepted pay rate is too high.
- You did not professionally answer any of the questions that I asked in the interview.

<u>MAYBE:</u> I would *consider* you for a position with the company. But with so many other *great* applicants and only a few positions available, you probably would not be selected.

- You are somewhat professional in your appearance, etiquette and attitude.
- You have a clean criminal background record. Or, what is on your record does not violate our company policy.
- You have a High School Diploma or GED.
- You have an Honorable or "Under Honorable Conditions" discharge from the military.

- You have a fair to good work history. Or if you have been a student or at home wife and mother you did not *fully* convince me that you have the qualities that an employer is looking for and that you can commit to the structure of the workplace.
- You have some flexibility in the shifts and/or days that you are able to work.
- You are flexible with the pay rate.
- You have satisfactory responses to the questions that I asked in the interview.

<u>YES:</u>   I would *definitely* consider you for a position.

- You are professional in your appearance, etiquette and attitude.
- You have a clean criminal background record. Or, what is on your record does not violate our company policy.
- You have a High School Diploma or GED.
- You have an Honorable or "Under Honorable Conditions" discharge from the military.
- You have a solid work history. Or if you have been a student or at home wife and mother you *did* convince me that you have the qualities that an employer is looking for and that you can commit to the structure of the workplace.
- You are flexible in the shifts and/or days that you are able to work.
- You are flexible with the pay rate.
- You have great responses to the questions that I ask you in the interview.

Now, with all that detailed, please know that the selection of employees is never black and white. There is always room for grey in every decision. I have selected many applicants that may have a poor work history, but have met so many of the other criteria that I am looking for that I still am willing to make an exception. I always let them know that on paper, or the initial impression may not make them appear to be a solid employee, but I am willing to open a door and let them prove themselves. Some have blown me away and become great, long lasting employees while others have come in one door and out the other. With the economy the way it is, most employers do not have an abundance of openings that they can use to give someone the opportunity to prove themselves. If you have any of the issues in the "NO" or "MAYBE" category that you cannot change, accentuate the qualities in the categories that *could* increase your E-Factor and get you the job. Next to manners and professional etiquette and attitude, flexibility in the shift and days that you are able to work in addition to being open to that company's starting pay rate go a long way in the decision and selection process.

Selecting someone for a position has been equated to the dating scene. You know the moment a person enters the room if they are someone you would be interested in getting to know better. So too the selection process for a job has that first impression moment that you get to win over the interviewer with your personality, education, experience and/or willingness to learn. You only have one chance to make a great impression. Do not waste it by disregarding all of the advice that I have given you throughout this book. If you fail in the interview, you will not be considered for a position with the company. It does not matter how persistent you are in following up on the status of your application. Coming into the office or calling excessively to check on the status of application is a waste of time. If you fail to impress me in the application/interview process, I am *not* going to select you.

While you are out looking for a job, because a potential employer may be calling at any time, make sure that you answer the phone professionally at all times. If you have a voicemail message that has more music than message or if the message sounds seductive or silly, you should definitely change it to a very basic message that sounds professional. This may seem like over-kill and that your personal message style reflects who you are. Everything counts when you are trying to get a job so change the message back to how you like it *after* you get the job.

If you have had a difficult time on your job search and have done many of the things that I have said *not* to do, I can venture to guess that *that* is the reason why you are not getting any job offers. Do not be discouraged, the good news is that you can always go to another employer or reapply with the same employer using the knowledge that you now have. My suggestion is that if you are attempting to reapply you should come back no sooner than six months to do so. You need enough time to pass, so if you made a bad first impression they will have long forgotten. That means, start from scratch. Do not say "I already filled out an application…can you look for it"? We do not want to take the time to go through hundreds of applications to look for your old application. Plus, your old application may have notes on it regarding your Employability Factor from their first encounter with you and, if it is not favorable, you want a fresh start.

The Interview
Do's & Don'ts

- **Do** remember your manners and professional etiquette and attitude.
- **Do** be ready, while waiting for the interview, for the Human Resource Manager to call your name at any moment.
- **Do** extend your hand and offer a firm (not hard) handshake.
- **Do** sit up straight in the chair and make sure that your body language is not sloppy, slouching or too laid back.
- **Do** look the interviewer in the eyes.
- **Do** be prepared to answer questions in the interview.
- **Do** make sure that your answering machine message sounds professional.
- **Don't** eat, drink, talk on the phone, or start reading a book or newspaper while waiting to be interviewed.
- **Don't** eat the candy.

CHAPTER 6

RULES, REGULATIONS & HARD WORK

Estee Lauder

Josephine Esther Mentzer lived above her father's hardware store in Corona, a section of Queens in New York City. She started her cosmetic enterprise by selling home made skin creams made by her uncle. Her product was not necessarily any better than those that were already on the market but she was simply a much better sales person and had more ambition than most. In the 1960's, after Galeries Lafayette in Paris declined to carry her perfume, she deliberately spilled a bottle on the floor. So many customers inquired abut the scent that the store was soon forced to place an order with her. Pioneering other unconventional tactics, such as free samples and gifts with purchases, Lauder built a cosmetic empire that became one of the world's leading manufacturers of skin-care products, makeup and fragrance. Her company is now worth an estimated 10 billion dollars. Concerning how she parlayed selling a home made skin cream into a multi billion dollar company she stated "I never *dreamed* of success, I worked hard for it."

Rules, Regulations & Hard Work

Many people make every effort to get a job but put absolutely no effort into keeping the job. Once you get the job, it is important that you do the best you can to keep the job. This is usually totally dependant upon, with the exception of a company downsizing or going out of business, your willingness to follow the company's rules and regulations *and* your work ethic. "Rules and regulations" are those company policies that if you violate will get you fired. Every company has their own polices regarding workplace rules and regulations. There may be some variances due to the nature of business that the company runs, but many policy standards are the same no matter who you work for. Standard company policies include the following:

ATTENDANCE

Not only should you be on time, it is to your benefit to always plan on being at least ten to fifteen minutes early. This way you can get in and get situated, put up belongings, make last minute phone calls, use the bathroom before you must report for work. Having a history for being on time will help you in dealing with your manager when you do have those rare occasions when the bus runs late, the car gets a flat, the alarm does not go off or you have any other life issue that slows you down from getting to work on time. No supervisor wants to loose a good employee. If you develop the reputation for being punctual and dependable, they will want to work with you as best they can. We all can have "issues" that could, if we allow it, prevent us from getting to work on time or to work at all for that matter. Most companies will try and work with you, at least for a short time, to resolve any conflicts that you may have that affect your attendance. Developing a pattern and reputation for tardiness and absenteeism is hard to overcome as you move forward with any company and will ultimately get you fired.

TIME KEEPING

Keep accurate records of the time that you work. If you falsify the records to appear as if you have worked more hours than you actually have in order to be paid a little more while working a little less, this is viewed as theft. You may be able to get away with it one or two times, but I guarantee that if a manager does not catch you a co-worker will tell on you and you will be out the door before you know it. The little bit of money that you could have gained by falsifying your time sheet is not worth the fact that you will be out of a job with *no* money and right back into the long and involved job search.

PROFESSIONAL DEMEANOR & WORKPLACE VIOLENCE

Professionalism is expected at all times while you are at work. Most companies have a zero tolerance policy when it comes to professional demeanor. That means…yes, your co-workers, supervisors, managers, customers/clients may (probably will) be frustrating at times. You *must* keep your cool! If you talk back, use profanity, argue and yell, or physically fight while on the job with a supervisor, manager, coworker or customer/client you will be fired. Saying that the other person provoked you usually will not help your case because it is still expected, no matter what the situation, that you remain professional. If you can think logically and remain calm at that point of frustration in the situation, you can then make a formal complaint against the other person for their behavior and let *their* job and income be in jeopardy and not yours.

DRUGS

The use of any drug (yes, this includes alcohol) while on your shift is unacceptable. And anything taken prior to your shift that either affects your performance or is detected by a co-worker or customer/client may also get you fired. I have had countless people fail the pre-qualifying drug test. I have had countless others fail the random drug test. Do not risk losing your job, your income, your reputation, your family and your life. If it is what you do to "relax", find another way to ease your mind. If it is a true addiction, you should seek professional help.

THEFT

Let me define what would be considered workplace theft so that there are no questions as to what behavior would not only get you fired, but may also get you criminally prosecuted. This could include everything from office supplies to anything that your company sells (food, apparel, computers, etc.). Don't fall into the trap of "They won't miss it", "It's just *one* pair of pants" or "It's just *one* lap top computer". Most companies have some sort of program set in place to monitor internal theft. This may be through inventory audits or hidden cameras. If you are terminated for theft and you are prosecuted and found guilty, upon looking for another job you have just further limited the opportunity of being hired by another company due to your criminal background record.

SEXUAL HARASSMENT

This would involve any situation where you would make a person uncomfortable because of unprofessional language and/or advances. This could involve crude jokes, persistent flirtation or unwanted physical contact.

If you offend someone in the workplace and they take it to management, you may get fired for sexual harassment. I have seen many situations where both parties may start out being mutually flirtatious and once one party no longer wants to continue the flirtation and expresses so, if the other party continues with unwanted flirtation, this would be considered sexual harassment. It is in your best interest to avoid any situation that could later be considered harassing. My suggestion is to watch your language and avoid dating co-workers as this could open up Pandora's Box.

SLEEPING ON THE JOB

Taking a "nap" or even "resting" in a manner that gives the appearance of sleeping will get you fired. I know that many people work two jobs or go to school or have children and this can drain most of your energy before you even get to work. But in order to keep your job, stay awake and alert by keeping busy, walking around or drinking a cup of coffee. Do anything other than putting yourself in a position that will cause you to fall asleep and lose your job.

Do not fall into the trap of lowering your standards because your co-workers are slack. You may get caught violating the rules and regulations and get fired and they may never get caught. Once you are terminated, you cannot say "Everybody is doing it"! That excuse does not hold water. You are grown and should know better. If you know better, do better. In this present economy, do everything that you can to keep your job.

While you are in the training period of your new job, I recommend that you bring paper and pen so that you can take notes and refer back to your notes once you no longer have the trainer looking over your shoulder and directing your every move. Whether you are a waitress, receptionist or computer specialist you are going to have to take notes. Doing so will help you assume your job responsibilities efficiently and avoid the situation of having to ask your trainer or supervisor "Now how do I do that again...I forgot?" or not asking and just plain doing it wrong makes all the difference in their level of respect, trust and consideration of you for future opportunities within the company.

I have seen good work ethics open doors in a company that should technically be filled by someone with a degree and/or more experience. Once in a company, you can create opportunities for advancement. The best way to do this is to always be professional in your appearance, attitude and etiquette. Have a strong work ethic. Be a leader in your morale and willingness to work together as a team with your co-workers. Take advantage of any internal training that the company may offer. I have seen ordinary people receive extraordinary opportunities to succeed because of these very reasons and *not* their college degree. Not that a college degree is insignificant. But for the millions of people that do not have the opportunity to obtain one, there is hope for opportunities and success based upon your hard work and professionalism. Both my husband and I started out in entry-level positions within a large company. Neither one of us had a formal degree but we committed do doing the very things that I have instructed you on throughout this book and both of us eventually moved into management positions.

Your opportunities for advancement may not be limited to the particular company you will be working for. I have passed out my business card to many people working in the mall, fast food restaurants, doctor's offices etc. because they have a professional appearance and have great customer service skills which makes me confident that they would be an asset to my company. So keep this in mind…you have no idea who you are dealing with when you are on the job and you have no idea when better opportunities may present themselves. So be professional, work hard, offer *great* customer service and you too can move up the ladder of success.

Rules, Regulations & Hard Work
Do's & Don'ts

- **Do** arrive at work on time everyday.
- **Do** take notes during your training period
- **Do** keep accurate records of your time.
- **Do** use professional language at all times.
- **Do** ask questions, cross-train and learn as much as possible about all positions.
- **Do** dress professionally.
- **Do** offer great customer service.
- **Don't** use profanity.
- **Don't** get into a physical fight.
- **Don't** verbally threaten anyone.
- **Don't** use drugs of any kind.
- **Don't** steal *anything* from your job.
- **Don't** tell dirty jokes that could offend someone listening.
- **Don't** make unwanted or even *wanted* sexual advances while working.
- **Don't** sleep on the job.

CHAPTER 7

CREATING & MAINTAINING A BUDGET

Truett Cathy

Samuel Truett Cathy, founder and chairman of the fast food restaurant chain Chik-fil-A, was born in Eatonton, Georgia in 1921. His father had a farming business that failed and the family of eight struggled to survive. They took in eight boarders to make ends meet in a single-family one bathroom house. The family's unfortunate financial circumstances laid the foundation for Cathy's strong work ethic as he later stated that "Growing up poor in a boarding house introduced me to hard work and taught me the value of diligent labor". At the age of eight he began buying six packs of Coca Cola for 25 cents and then selling individual bottles door-to-door for 5 cents each. At the age of nine he opened a soft drink stand in his front yard. At the age of ten he sold newspapers door to door. At the age of eleven he helped a friend with a paper route and at the age of twelve he had a paper route of his own. In his twenties, he opened his first restaurant and the rest is history. With over seven hundred restaurants and one billion dollars in sales, Truett Cathy is another great example of triumph over tragedy through perseverance and the willingness to work hard.

Creating & Maintaining a Budget

Now that you have all of the information that you need to get a job and keep a job, it is time to evaluate your financial situation and your future. Getting a job is the first step towards reaching your goals, but making wise choices with your money is the key to building the strong foundation that you will need to reach those goals. You may have no problem when it comes to money. You pay your bills on time. You do not buy on impulse. You live within your means. You do not compete with the Jones'. You have not "maxed out" your credit cards. You pay off your debt. You have a budget that works for your household and you stick to it *and* you even have a savings account. That's great!! But for most of us, we need a little help.

I know that for some of you reading this, you may want to close the book right now and just be happy getting a job. It can be emotionally painful to take an honest look at where you stand in relation to your finances. I know this feeling all too well. It is as if something grips your heart and mind and tells you to bury your head in the sand and it will all go away. After years of trying that approach you will, like me, raise your head up one day and realize that not only has it not gone away, it has gotten worse. I encourage you to resist the impulse to emotionally hide from your financial situation. If you continue with this chapter you will not feel overwhelmed you will feel empowered. For once in your life you will see the light at the end of the tunnel and have hope for financial freedom. So take a deep breath and keep on reading.

The first step is creating a budget. Having a budget simply means customizing a system of spending that works well for your household. Every Fortune 500 Company must run on a budget if it is going to remain successful. They have quarterly reports to analyze how the company is doing financially. If there is a hint that at the end of their fiscal year they are in jeopardy of a financial loss and not a profit, they immediately address every area of their company's expenditures. They would then eliminate or scale back those expenditures that are not vital to the functioning of the company as a whole. Your household needs the same attention in order to be financially successful. For example, if when you get that job, you eat out for lunch every day at work spending $10 dollars a day, multiplying this by five days equals $50 dollars a week. Multiply this by 52 weeks and you have spent a grand total of $2,600 in one year just for lunch. With a little planning, you could easily prepare your lunch at home for less than 1/4 the cost of this and save over $1,500 dollars a year. That would be an additional $1,500 dollars in your budget for other bills, savings or something special like a family vacation.

Your weakness may not be eating out. It may be shopping or entertainment. In any case, it is time to take a good hard look at where you spend your money. This will assist you greatly in creating a budget for your household. Where you need to modify your spending is going to be unique to your situation. Your budget depends on your income, your debt, your monthly expenses and your goals. It is designed to help keep you within certain financial parameters so that there is not one dollar unaccounted for nor one dollar wasted.

Aren't you tired of hearing about recording artists who go bankrupt? Or, people who win the lottery losing it all due to lavish lifestyles? With all of that money, they lack the ability to implement and monitor a budget in their life so they lose everything and have no record of where it went. It takes wisdom and discipline to create and follow a budget. Whether you are making minimum wage or have a six-figure salary, you need a budget. You need to be aware of how much money is coming in and how much money is going out *and* where it is going.

Let's get to it! You will find a worksheet to assist you at the end of this chapter. You can also purchase a financial planner from any office supply store or you can customize your own. Use whatever works best for you. Whatever the format may be, the necessary information is the same.

1. Determine your monthly household income. (I do understand that you may be reading this *prior* to finding a job. If that is the case, do *not* stop reading! Understanding how to implement and maintain a budget is so important that although you do not have a job yet, you will know exactly what to do with every paycheck once you do.) This includes money from a job, alimony, child support, etc. If you have a two-income family, include both salaries. Always use your net income (total after taxes) in determining this amount. If you are using the budget tables provided at the end of this chapter, place your monthly income dollar amount in the Household Income category.

2 . Make an itemized list of all of your Set Monthly Expenses. That is, those expenses that are a relatively consistent amount from month to month. Such as mortgage/rent, utilities, car payment, insurance (home/life/car/health/etc.), current credit cards, current loans, education, day care, child support, alimony, etc.

3. Deduct this amount from Household Income.

4. After detailing your Household Income and Set Monthly Expenses, you will have an estimate of how much of your income every month you can allocate towards "Variable Monthly Expenses". "Variable Monthly Expenses" are those areas in which you can modify your spending. This would include toiletries, food, eating out, entertainment, beauty parlor/barber shop, gifts, etc. These are the areas of your day to day living that, if need be, you could scale back and save money.

Seeing your income and spending detailed in front of you for the first time may be a little overwhelming. Especially if you never realized what a gap there was between the money that you have coming in and the money you have going out. Do not faint. Ignorance is *not* bliss! This is a challenge that you can overcome! Take a deep breath and let's press on together.

In order to be truly successful in your finances you must not only *create* a household budget you must *maintain* a household budget. This means breaking old habits and implementing new habits. It took a long time to get into financial distress and it will take some time to move into financial success. Determination and consistency are the keys to wealth. You must monitor and detail in writing all of your spending in order to develop a budget that works well for your household. This can seem tedious and monotonous. You may start out strong and then fall off in your tracking of your spending. Do not throw in the towel, simply start over and keep working at this until it becomes a way of life. This is not simply a means of getting you out of debt it is a way for you to obtain and maintain wealth and leave an inheritance for the generations that come after you. Anyone who has ever been financially successful will tell you that the foundation for building wealth is having a sound budget. That is, knowing how much money you have as your bottom line and maximizing that money by allocating it out to the right areas. If you cannot implement a budget for your current situation, how will you ever maintain a budget when you buy that dream home or start your own business?

We all want to run with our finances and yet many of us have never learned how to crawl. If you desire more from your life financially, this is where you must start … creating a household budget. It is my hope that you comprehend the necessity of implementing a household budget and with all seriousness and diligence maintain it. With this in place, you will have a strong foundation on which to build your present goals and future dreams.

Creating & Maintaining a Budget
Do's & Don'ts

- **Do** take the time to create your personalized household budget.
- **Do** keep accurate records of your daily spending.
- **Do** be honest with yourself about your current financial situation.
- **Do** look for areas in your spending that you can save money.
- **Do** re-read the biographies throughout the book and be encouraged.
- **Don't** be discouraged about your present financial state.
- **Don't** overextend your credit.
- **Don't** try to keep up with the Jones'.

MONTHLY HOUSEHOLD BUDGET

HOUSEHOLD INCOME

SOURCE   AMOUNT

_____   _____

_____   _____

_____   _____

SET MONTHLY EXPENSES

ITEM   DUE DATE   AMOUNT

_____   _____   _____

_____   _____   _____

_____   _____   _____

_____   _____   _____

_____   _____   _____

_____   _____   _____

_____   _____   _____

_____   _____   _____

_____   _____   _____

_____   _____   _____

_____   _____   _____

_____   _____   _____

VARIABLE MONTHLY EXPENSES

ITEM   AMOUNT

_____   _____

_____   _____

_____   _____

_____   _____

_____   _____

_____   _____

_____   _____

_____   _____

_____**TOTAL MONTHLY INCOME**

_____**SET MONTHLY EXPENSES**

_____**BALANCE REMAINING FOR VARIABLE MONTHLY EXPENSES**

CONCLUSION

I have given you all of the helpful hints and pointers concerning your Employability Factor that five years of experience in a Human Resource Department has afforded me. I do hope that you can walk away with at least one suggestion that can benefit your job search as well as your present life and future endeavors. My desire for your life exceeds you just getting a job. Although I do understand that without a job to take care of your immediate financial needs, trying to look too far in the future can seem like an impossible task. It can be hard to set goals for your life five or ten years from now when today you are on the verge of being evicted, have children to care for, have bill collectors calling, or are so consumed with the pressures and responsibilities of your day to day life that planning for the future appears to be a luxury and not a necessity.

My life has been filled with many of the same trials that you may be currently facing. I have been through unemployment, homelessness and a million things in between. I know what it is like being unemployed and I know what it is like having three jobs. I have washed windows, thrown newspapers and pawned jewelry to make ends meet. I have gotten where I am through hard work, determination and a desire to want more for my life and those whom I love. I am not highly educated, I did not have any "connections", I did not know how to "network", I lacked basic computer skills and even a professional wardrobe. I am an ordinary woman who has opened doors of opportunity by my work ethic, willingness to learn and earnest desire to want more out of my life. From there I used that experience and inside information to write this book to hopefully open doors of opportunity for you as well. If it can happen for me it can happen for *anyone*.

If I can leave you with one final thought it would be this…we are all ordinary people who can make extraordinary things happen in our life if we set goals, diligently pursue and work hard to realize those goals and believe that all things are possible to those who, when their back is up against a wall, press towards something greater than the situation that they find themselves in. I can speak emphatically that you too like Madame C.J. Walker, Colin Powell, Alonzo Herndon, Debbie Fields, Oprah Winfrey, Estee Lauder, Truett Cathy and many, many others can be a person whose life is made to be an example for the generations to come on how to overcome adversity, trials, discrimination and lack…lack of money, lack of education, lack of support from family and friends. Having a vision that is greater than your present situation along with willingness to work hard to see it come to pass will change your life forever. And when it happens, because it will, share your life experience, challenges and triumphs, with others so that they too may be encouraged to dream new dreams, redefine goals and work hard to see the vision come to pass.

ABOUT THE AUTHOR

Jill Russell is an experienced Human Resource Manager and Recruiter. That experience, coupled with a sincere desire to help those who are seeking employment obtain a job, led her to offer presentations at various Atlanta area Workforce Development Agencies on what employers are looking for *and* looking at during the selection and hiring process – the Employability Factor. She has put all of her insight and inside information in this book in a straight forward, tell-it-like-it-is approach in the hope that it would be the key to success for anyone struggling with "Don't call us we'll call you".